∝

Unmasking
Mother Teresa's
Critics

D0711323

Bill Donohue

Unmasking Mother Teresa's Critics

SOPHIA INSTITUTE PRESS
Manchester, New Hampshire

Sophia Institute Press
Box 5284, Manchester, NH 03108
1-800-888-9344

SophiaInstitute.com

Sophia Institute Press® is a registered trademark of Sophia Institute.

Library of Congress Cataloging-in-Publication Data

Names: Donohue, William A., 1947- author.
Title: Unmasking Mother Teresa's critics / Bill Donohue.
Description: Manchester, New Hampshire : Sophia Institute Press, 2016. |
    Includes bibliographical references.
Identifiers: LCCN 2016023106 | ISBN 9781622823758 (pbk. : alk. paper)
Subjects: LCSH: Teresa, Mother, 1910-1997.
Classification: LCC BX4406.5.Z8 D66 2016 | DDC 271/.97—dc23 LC
record available at https://lccn.loc.gov/2016023106

First printing

For Donald Cardinal Wuerl

Contents

Acknowledgments

My love for Mother Teresa grew considerably while researching and writing this book. Conversely, my displeasure with her most famous critics grew commensurately: their dishonesty is appalling. It is one thing to point out her shortcomings, quite another to misrepresent her work and disparage her efforts. After reading their failed accounts, I am convinced more than ever that Mother Teresa is a role model for the entire human race.

I would like to thank Charlie McKinney, president of Sophia Institute Press, for his strong interest in this book. Nora Malone, my editor, is as easy to work with as she is competent.

Unmasking Mother Teresa's Critics

Many thanks to Bernadette Brady-Egan, vice president of the Catholic League, for her encouragement. Rick Hinshaw, the director of communications, helped to edit the volume, as did two policy analysts, Katelynn Bernhardi and Don Lauer. Their commitment and goodwill is very much appreciated.

Finally, I would like to thank my family, Valerie, Caryn, Paul, Caitlin, and Tara for their steady support.

❦

Unmasking
Mother Teresa's
Critics

Introduction

Father Brian Kolodiejchuk, a priest in the Missionaries of Charity, was delighted when the Vatican announced that Mother Teresa would be canonized; he is her postulator, the priest who took up her cause for sainthood. "I've been working on it for 17 years," he said, "since 1999, so there's a sense of coming to a happy conclusion."[1] Pope John Paul II beatified Mother Teresa in 2003.

Father Kolodiejchuk was not the only person who was happy with the news: Mother Teresa is beloved by

---

[1] Edward Pentin, "Mother Teresa to Be Canonized on Sept. 4," *National Catholic Register*, April 3–16, 2016.

hundreds of millions all over the world, drawing the affection of those of many religions and even those who have no religious affiliation. But as we shall see, even someone of Mother Teresa's towering stature is not universally loved. Her critics will be given due consideration and evaluation.

The Vatican takes the cause of sainthood seriously. With regard to Mother Teresa, the inquiry collected thirty-five thousand pages of documentation and testimony and interviewed many witnesses; the probe took two years to complete. The investigation also established a twelve-member episcopal team, known as devil's advocates, whose purpose was to challenge the claims of those lobbying for sainthood. Even Mother Teresa's most notorious critic, Christopher Hitchens, was summoned for testimony.

"By blood, I am Albanian. By citizenship, an Indian. By faith, I am a Catholic nun. As to my calling, I belong to the world. As to my heart, I belong entirely to the Heart of Jesus."[2] The future St. Teresa of

---

[2] "Mother Teresa of Calcutta (1910–1997)," http://www. vatican.va/.

Kolkata (formerly Calcutta), was not boasting, only telling the truth.

Born in Skopje (now part of Macedonia) on August 26, 1910, Agnes Gonxha Bojaxhiu (the future Mother Teresa) left home at the age of eighteen to join the Institute of the Blessed Virgin Mary, known in Ireland as the Sisters of Loreto; they had a community in India. She took the name Sister Mary Teresa, after St. Thérèse of Lisieux. She didn't stay long before leaving for India, arriving in Calcutta on January 6, 1929.

In 1946, Mother Teresa experienced what she said was a "call within a call," an inspiration to leave the Loreto convent and dedicate herself to the poor and the dying.[3] After moving to the slums, she received permission from the Vatican in 1950 to found the Missionaries of Charity. From then on she would commit herself to "the poorest of the poor."

She started with only thirteen members, yet as early as 1952 she opened the first Home for the Dying, one of her signature achievements. The nuns acquired

[3] Ibid.

medical care for the sick and offered comfort to the dying. Next she focused on those suffering from leprosy. Then she turned her attention to children, opening a home for orphans and the homeless; she named it Nirmala Shishu Bhavan (the Children's Home of the Immaculate Heart). Over time, hospices were founded in many nations, servicing the dispossessed and outcasts.

Chapter 1

"Discovering" Mother Teresa

Mother Teresa was a humble person who never sought the limelight. That being so, how did she come to the attention of the world? The credit goes to Malcolm Muggeridge.

Muggeridge was a British journalist who was well known to his countrymen for his writings and TV appearances. He was an independent-minded agnostic who opposed both contraception and abortion. In the 1920s, he took an assignment to India and eventually converted: he first became an Anglican and then in 1982 became a Catholic.

In 1968, Muggeridge's boss at the BBC asked him to interview an Indian nun who was visiting in

London. Kathryn Spink, one of Mother Teresa's biographers, described how it went:

> Mother Teresa was very nervous in front of the camera and somewhat halting in speech. The interview was technically a disaster, so much so that the producers doubted for a while whether it was good enough for showing at all, except perhaps late at night.[4]

When the interview aired on a Sunday evening, the reaction was astonishing. Muggeridge was particularly impressed; he knew he had latched on to someone wholly unique. "This woman spoke to me as no one ever has, and I feel I must help her," he said. But it wasn't just the TV ratings that soared—letters and contributions came pouring in from all over the United Kingdom.[5]

Muggeridge was determined to follow up on his discovery, and in 1969 he succeeded in getting Mother

---

4 Kathryn Spink, *Mother Teresa: An Authorized Biography* (New York: HarperOne, 2011), 126.
5 Ibid., 126–27.

Teresa to sit down for a documentary, *Something Beautiful for God* (named after a book that Muggeridge wrote about her). He knew Calcutta well, but did not know what to expect when he arrived. He visited the Home for the Dying. "The home was overflowing with love," he observed, "and the love was luminous. God's invisible omnipresent love. A miracle."[6] This event had a dramatic effect on his life; it eventually led to his conversion to Catholicism.

[6] Ibid., 165.

Chapter 2

Mother Teresa's Critics Emerge

Although Muggeridge introduced Mother Teresa's
yeoman work to the world in the late 1960s, it was
not until the 1990s that anyone seriously sought to
challenge her reputation. Dr. Aroup Chatterjee was
among the first to do so.

In February of 1993, Chatterjee asked for a meeting with officials from Bandung Productions, a film
company owned by Tariq Ali, a writer and broad-
caster in England. Chatterjee wanted to discuss his
interest in doing a documentary on Mother Teresa.
Perturbed by the perception that his hometown of
Calcutta was known only for its horrible conditions
and its surplus of homeless persons—a perception

he attributed to Mother Teresa — he sought to alter that view. He eventually wrote a critical book about Mother Teresa, *The Final Verdict*.

Chatterjee leaned on Vanya Del Borgo to do most of the research for the documentary. Not being a media person, Chatterjee asked her if there was someone who shared his views and might be willing to present the film. She did some scratching around and named Christopher Hitchens, a British writer whom she had worked with in her days at the *Nation*, a left-wing journal based in New York City. After Del Borgo contacted Hitchens, he agreed to do the film.

The alliance ran into problems from the start. Although Hitchens did none of the research, he took command of the project as if he had. To be sure, he did the writing, but he also presented the documentary to the public as if it had been his idea all along.

Moreover, according to Chatterjee, he lied when he said that he edited the film and was involved in the post shooting. From then on, Chatterjee questioned his integrity, noting that since 1993, Hitchens "did his best to take every credit about this whole exposé."[7]

The first broadside against Mother Teresa occurred when Hitchens presented the documentary *Hell's Angels* on British TV in November 1994. This was the beginning of Hitchens' lifetime assault on her, portraying her as a dishonest person who associated with crooks and dictators, allowing the sick to die without adequate care.

Chatterjee, although no fan of Mother Teresa, was not only angered by the way Hitchens sought to take most of the credit for the film, but he blew up when he saw the final product. "I am not happy with how 'Hell's Angels' turned out, especially its slanderous and sensationalist approach," he said. "I have dissociated myself from the film."[8]

---

[7] Hemley Gonzalez, "Dr. Aroup Chatterjee and Hemley Gonzalez Discuss Mother Teresa, Christopher Hitchens and the Negligence and Fraud of the Catholic Nun," January 1, 2014, Stop the Missionaries of Charity, missionariesofcharity.wordpress.com.

[8] Catriona Crowe, "Under the Microscope, Mother Teresa: The Final Verdict," *Irish Times*, February 15, 2003.

Chatterjee was right about this. Indeed, the documentary turned out to be a hit job. None of the men, women, and children who were under the care of Mother Teresa were interviewed for the film. "Not a single person cared for by the Missionaries speaks on camera," notes William Doino Jr. Pointedly, Doino asks, "Was this because they had a far higher opinion of Blessed Teresa than Hitchens would permit in his film?"[9]

After Father Kolodiejchuk watched the documentary with a group of Missionaries of Charity sisters, they compared notes. They assessed how the film portrayed Mother Teresa compared with their own observations. He spoke for them when he concluded, "Wait a minute, this is partial—it's a twisting of things around."[10]

This is what propaganda films do: they blend truths with half-truths, mixing them with incredulous commentary and depictions. Because there is a veneer of plausibility to the presentation, some think it may

[9] William Doino Jr., "Mother Teresa and Her Critics," *First Things*, April 1, 2013, firstthings.com.

[10] Pentin, "Mother Teresa to Be Canonized."

be true. That is why such politically contrived films are so dangerous. To the undiscerning eye, fact and fiction bleed into each other, the effect of which is to distort reality.

Chapter 3

What's Driving the Attacks?

Almost all of Mother Teresa's critics have been non-believers or left-wing writers or activists, or both. This is not an accident: it's what drives them to attack her.

"What is the most counter-cultural message of the Gospel?" Father John J. Lombardi poses the question and provides a cogent answer: "Selflessness and suffering."[11] No one exemplified these two attributes better than Mother Teresa. Her critics do not dispute this observation, but for them there is nothing virtuous about these characteristics.

[11] William Donohue, *The Catholic Advantage: Why Health, Happiness, and Heaven Await the Faithful* (New York: Image, 2015), 69.

Unmasking Mother Teresa's Critics

Those who lack faith frequently lack a belief in altruism. So when someone is touted as an altruist, especially a person of faith, they look askance at the evidence. Even more objectionable in their secular eyes is the Catholic belief in redemptive suffering; they cannot comprehend how our suffering can be united with Christ's.

Similarly, those who harbor a collectivist ideology are skeptical, if not cynical, of attempts to help the poor that do not stem from government. Indeed, they see private, voluntary outreach programs as a deterrent to statist prescriptions. And nothing is more objectionable than efforts that emanate from religious quarters; in their eyes, that really stymies government welfare programs.

It would be unfair to say that Mother Teresa objected to government programs that serve the poor. Her preference, however, was to provide personal care, establishing a relationship between the caregiver and the needy. Catholic social teaching stresses commitment not only to the poor but also to the principle of subsidiarity: those closest to the problem are best able to address it. Mother Teresa took this as her cue to deliver personal care to the sick and the dying.

Mother Teresa, of course, is the embodiment of these convictions. She was an altruist supreme, one who drew from Jesus all the resources she needed to serve "the poorest of the poor." Just as important, she often noted how she was able to unite her sufferings, and those of others, to the sufferings of Jesus on the Cross.

For all these reasons, she attracted a small, but determined, band of critics. Although they are seriously outnumbered by those who have recounted Mother Teresa's stunning achievements, they cannot be ignored. Indeed, they need to be challenged.

Chapter 4

Christopher Hitchens

No one is more famous for lashing out at Mother Teresa than Christopher Hitchens. I confronted him many times, at formal debates and on television. I admired his intellect and wit but had a low opinion of him as a scholar: he was not concerned about facts and was prone to sloppy research. While we disagreed about most things, we had two interests in common: he was pro-life (although that didn't stop him from bashing Mother Teresa on this issue), and he understood the threat that radical Islam posed to the West. No matter; our relationship was choppy at best.

Hitchens accused Mother Teresa of "deceiving us." She was, in his estimation, a "religious fundamentalist, a political operative, a primitive sermonizer and ac-complice of worldly secular powers." She was also "a demagogue" who kept company with "frauds, crooks and exploiters."[12] That was the central conclusion he came to in his book, *The Missionary Position: Mother Teresa in Theory and Practice*.

When an author makes serious accusations against serious persons, he is obliged to have his facts in order. Hitchens didn't even try. His essay contained not one piece of evidence. There were no footnotes, no end-notes, no citations of any kind. This is not scholarship.

I often asked him why anyone should believe his unsupported opinions, rejecting the accounts of ev-eryone else. Indeed, I told him at our debate at the Union League Club in New York City in 2000 that if he were a student of mine in college, I would assign him an F for his work.[13]

---

[12] William Donohue, "Hating Mother Teresa," *Catalyst*, March 1996; available online at catholicleague.org.

[13] Donohue-Hitchens debate, March 23, 2000, New York City, posted at Catholic League for Religious and Civil Rights (http://www.catholicleague.org/donohue-hitch-ens-debate-online/) and on YouTube.

Hitchens was both an atheist and a socialist; he was also self-destructive, dying prematurely at the age of sixty-two. Suffice it to say that he had nothing in common with Mother Teresa, save for his professed interest in the poor. But unlike her, he did nothing to ameliorate their condition. Instead, he settled for socialist prescriptions, policies that, if anything, make the poor poorer. The irony was, I informed him, that Mother Teresa made her name by cleaning up after the conditions that ideologues like him helped to create.

In England, Hitchens wrote for the *New Statesman*, and when he came to New York he landed a job writing for the *Nation*, a magazine that stood staunchly behind Joseph Stalin. It should be noted that his father was a gunrunner for Old Joe, proving once again that the apple doesn't fall far from the tree. Hitchens was a good foot soldier for the left, opposing the deployment of cruise missiles and Pershing missiles in Europe. He sided with the Marxist thugs in Nicaragua, the Sandinistas, and opposed the American liberation of Grenada.

Although Hitchens' socialist convictions help to explain his opposition to Mother Teresa's private-sector approach to the poor, it does not adequately explain his strong hostility to her. To understand that, we need to appreciate the depth of his atheism.

Today, there is a price to be paid if someone is known as a bigot, but this is not universally true. It is acceptable to be anti-Catholic, and this is especially true among elites. That is why they tolerate, if not contribute to, Catholic bashing in the arts, education, government, the media, and the entertainment world. Hitchens merits a top spot in this lineup.

He opened our 2000 debate by saying, "I might have to admit for debate purposes that when religion is attacked in this country that the Catholic Church comes in for little more than its fair share." He confessed, without a trace of embarrassment, "I may say that I probably contributed somewhat to that and I am not ashamed of my part in it."[14]

Hitchens was not content to take issue with Mother Teresa's beliefs and practices—he had to attack her personally. He called her the "ghoul of Calcutta," saying that her opposition to contraception and abortion "sounds grotesque when uttered by an elderly virgin";

[14] Ibid.

he also called her "a presumable virgin."[15] Several of his *ad hominem* cracks were made about her looks.

On November 2, 2009, Hitchens accused Mother Teresa of making the poor worse off, and as a result, "it's a shame there is no hell for [the] bitch to go to." I jumped all over him for that remark, and he got back to me the same day. "The first thing to say is that I felt remorse for employing the word 'bitch' as soon as it was out of my mouth."[16] I accepted the apology. I also offered to buy him a drink (something else we had in common). He said he looked forward to downing a few pints, but unfortunately he was diagnosed with cancer about six months later; we never did imbibe together. Christopher died on December 15, 2011.

[15] See Donohue, "Hating Mother Teresa," and Christopher Hitchens, "Mother Teresa and Me," *Vanity Fair*, February 8, 1995, 40.

[16] "Donohue-Hitchens Settle Dispute," November 5, 2009; the news release is available online at catholicleague.org.

Chapter 5

Aroup Chatterjee and Hemley Gonzalez

Aroup Chatterjee is not as well known as Christopher Hitchens, but as already disclosed, he was the man behind the first public attack on her: it was his idea to do the documentary *Hell's Angels*.

A self-proclaimed atheist, he took issue with the number of persons whom Mother Teresa claimed to serve. Yet he offered no proof that her figures were wrong. The best he could do was to criticize journalists for not checking her statistics. He offered his own figures, concluding that her numbers were inflated. But on what basis? He admitted that his figures were an estimate. Which begs the question: Why should we believe that his numbers are more accurate than Mother Teresa's?

In 2002, seven years after Hitchens published *The Missionary Position*, Chatterjee released his book, *The Final Verdict*. The reviews were horrible, even among those who were ideologically in his camp. The *Irish Times* ripped it: "The book is full of misprints, appalling syntax, missing words, and repetition."[17] The *Mirror* of London faulted it, warning readers, "One has to approach the book with caution because his total antipathy to Mother Teresa is palpable throughout the book."[18]

Most people were pleased that Mother Teresa had such a great relationship with Pope John Paul II, but to critics such as Chatterjee, this is proof of something sinister. He argues that their orthodoxy led to her becoming the Vatican's ideal missionary, moving about the world to promote "spiritual work" for the poor.[19]

---

[17] Crowe, "Under the Microscope."

[18] Niall Moonan, "Saint or Sinner? Scurrilous New Book Claims Mother Teresa Lied about Saving Flood Victims," *Mirror*, October 9, 2003, 10.

[19] Krishna Dutta, "Saint of the Gutters with Friends in High Places," *Times Higher Education Supplement*, May 16, 2003.

In Chatterjee's mind, Mother Teresa's travels to Communist countries and Muslim-run nations were more self-serving than altruistic. His cynicism is so deep that even Mother Teresa's most innocuous outreach programs are subjected to searing scrutiny. This only proves that once an ideologue has his mind made up, no amount of hard data will change it.

Hemley Gonzalez is a migrant from Cuba who settled in Miami. A militant secularist, he worked with Mother Teresa as a volunteer for two months.

Like so many other critics of Mother Teresa, Gonzalez accuses the Missionaries of Charity of failing to adopt more progressive measures to fight poverty, e.g., promoting birth control and abortion. He blames their failure to do so on their "worship of superstition and sadism," adding that they also suffer from "mental illness." He also brands the religious order as "nothing less than a glorified cult."[20]

These are serious charges. They would take on considerable weight if they were offered by a prominent

---

[20] Mike Kuhlenbeck, "The Humanist Interview with Hemley Gonzalez," December 20, 2013, thehumanist.com.

mental-health professional, but Gonzalez holds no such credentials: he is a high school graduate who pursued a career in real estate.

After his stint with Mother Teresa, Gonzalez left Calcutta for a while, and then came back to found Responsible Charity, a program to help the sick. He bragged about how his outfit would really make a difference in their lives. Initially, he funded emergency relief efforts and organized clothing drives. But it takes the stamina and determination of Mother Teresa to stay the course, something he failed to do.

In 2012, Responsible Charity had a new mission: it took up the cause of Slutwalk. Gonzalez and his crew walked the streets of Calcutta protesting the perception that women who dress like sluts are making themselves candidates for rape.[21] Two years later, Gonzalez joined Slutwalk's new constituency—lesbian, gay, bisexual, and transgender. They marched through the streets of Calcutta educating the residents about their new agenda. "Everybody has a right

[21] "Slutwalk Hits Kolkata Streets," *Times of India*, May 25, 2012.

to be who they are irrespective of gender.... It's about being human."[22]

Mother Teresa, of course, never departed from her commitment to the poor, the sick, and the dying. Gonzalez's only legacy is his "STOP the Missionaries of Charity" campaign. It was a monumental failure.

After reading about each other online, Chatterjee and Gonzalez finally met in Calcutta a few years ago. It turned out to be quite a moment. They congratulated themselves on seeing what a fraud Mother Teresa was and how they outsmarted everyone else.

"People at the Vatican must be laughing their heads off," said Chatterjee, "thinking they really struck gold in Calcutta." Gonzalez replied, "The Vatican is a huge machine and people fail to realize the extent to which the Vatican's financial powers and influence can reach. They created this brand, Mother Teresa has been manufactured out of Calcutta and sold to the masses."[23]

---

[22] "Kolkata's Slutwalk Demand Humane Society," *IANS-English*, March 21, 2014.

[23] Gonzalez, "Dr. Aroup Chatterjee and Hemley Gonzalez Discuss Mother Teresa."

If Mother Teresa were nothing more than a useful commodity created in Rome to advance its power and prestige, surely some of her followers, or patients, would have noticed. But none did. To Chatterjee and Gonzalez, this is of no consequence, and that is because they really believe they possess gnostic-like insights: they can see things that other mere mortals cannot.

If these two sages exhibited only arrogance, that wouldn't be so bad. But there is a venal streak in them, as well. Chatterjee is appalled that so many people see Calcutta as a destitute city, and he blames Mother Teresa for that perception. He is not willing simply to disagree—he demands that the Missionaries of Charity offer a public apology. Moreover, there should be "financial compensation to the city for causing harm, financial damage, and damage to business and tourism." Accordingly, he says, "some retribution is due."[24]

According to the logic of these two atheists, if Mother Teresa's care for the sick and the dying is responsible for Calcutta's bad image, then cops in

[24] Ibid.

high-crime cities are responsible for their bad image. Perhaps we should demand that the police offer a public apology and provide financial compensation to the thugs they patrol. Come to think of it, morticians give funeral homes a bad name.

Chapter 6

Canadian Critics Strike

The latest critics of Mother Teresa of any note come from Canada. Three scholars, Serge Larivée and Geneviève Chénard of the University of Montreal and Carole Sénéchal of the University of Ottawa published an article in the March 2013 issue of *Studies in Religion/Sciences Religieuses* that attracted media attention. The piece, "The Dark Side of Mother Teresa," is not available in English (it was translated from the French for the Catholic League).[25]

[25] Serge Larivée, Geneviève Chénard, and Carole Sénéchal, "The Dark Side of Mother Teresa," *Studies in Religion/Sciences Religieuses* 42, no. 3 (March 2013): 319–345.

The authors were drawn to study Mother Teresa's accomplishments when they pursued documentation on the subject of altruism. They regard altruism as a myth, and it is a short leap from there to discounting the nun's work. They read a great deal of the literature on Mother Teresa but never visited the Missionaries of Charity to judge their work, nor did they interview any of the nuns, volunteers, or their subjects.

The authors do not hide their biases: they not only reject the teachings of the Catholic Church on sexuality; they deride them as well. They also ridicule Muggeridge for his "right wing catholic [sic] values," and Mother Teresa for discovering "how profitable mass media can be."[26]

Regarding the latter, they question whether "it is Mother Teresa who forced the press to notice her or if it was the press that forced Mother Teresa to endorse this role." As it turns out, they really aren't sure. But they readily accept the "myth of Mother Teresa" thesis that was promoted by Hitchens, concluding that "the myth has been effective and has

[26] Ibid., 325.

served the cause of Mother Teresa and that of the Vatican well."[27]

Why the derisive tone? The Canadian professors, like Mother Teresa's socialist critics, are troubled by her voluntarism in service to the poor. "Such a model of charity overshadow[s] the urgency of taking our collective responsibilities and getting organized with regards to social justice."[28] In other words, the more the nuns do to help the needy, the less pressure there is on the state to get involved. One might think this would be cause for celebration — especially since there is no substitute for one-on-one care — but to those who share the socialist vision, the nuns are a problem.

The authors are also appalled by Catholicism. "Mother Teresa always firmly opposed abortion, contraception and divorce." Why is this a problem? "If we think about it," they write, "opposition to abortion can only increase misery in Calcutta."[29]

Perhaps they did not think about it enough. Mother Teresa thought about it, and she concluded

[27] Ibid., 339.
[28] Ibid., 340.
[29] Ibid., 328.

that abortion means the certain death of innocents, some of whom experience excruciating misery in the womb. According to the logic of these Canadians, opposition to infanticide also increases misery in Calcutta: it means there will be more poor people living there, the kind of people who make Chatterjee embarrassed about his hometown.

Chapter 7

Consorting with the Rich and Famous

Anyone who has ever run a charity knows how difficult it is to raise money. Sometimes a generous donor comes along and provides funding. Those who are very successful in their fundraising pursuits may wind up meeting the rich and famous, and while most are ethically clean, some are not.

Should this matter? If so, it raises another question: Don't the recipients have a moral obligation to their clients to raise as much money as they possibly can, as long as it is obtained through legal means? Should we expect them to have their donors submit to a polygraph, proving their nobility? Most important, how well are the needy served by turning down funding that could help them?

Mother Teresa's fame brought her to the attention of many prominent persons in business and politics, most of whom were good people. But some were controversial. Her critics fault her for consorting with them.

For example, was it wrong for her to take money from British publisher Robert Maxwell? He embezzled millions from his employees' pension funds. If she knew that he had ripped off his own people to give to her, and she took his money anyway, that would be a problem. But that is not what happened. It was only *after* she accepted his donations and the money was spent that his criminal behavior was revealed. That is not a small difference.

Simon Leys is a distinguished Australian intellectual who has examined the charges made against Mother Teresa. He knows why her critics are upset with her: "She occasionally accepts the hospitality of crooks, millionaires, and criminals." His reply is devastating: "But it is hard to see why, as a Christian, she should be more choosy in this respect than her

Master, whose bad frequentations were notorious, and shocked all the Hitchenses of His time."[30]

If there is one donor who Mother Teresa's critics like to pounce on, it is Charles Keating. New York writer Murray Kempton minces no words: "The swindler Charles Keating gave her $1.25 million—most dubiously his own to give—and she rewarded him with the 'personalized crucifix' he doubtless found of sovereign use as an ornamental camouflage for his pirate flag."[31] If Kempton had something serious to say about this matter, he would not have had to resort to sarcasm.

The Keating canard was first introduced by Hitchens. Keating was sentenced to prison for his role in a scandal involving the United States Savings and Loan. But as with Maxwell, the money he gave to Mother Teresa was *prior* to his offense, and when it was revealed that he was a crook, the money had already been spent.

---

[30] Simon Leys, letter to the editor, *New York Review of Books*, September 19, 1996.

[31] Murray Kempton, "The Shadow Saint," *New York Review of Books*, July 11, 1996.

Hitchens also criticized Mother Teresa for writing a letter to Judge Lance Ito "seeking clemency for Mr. Keating." She did nothing of the sort. She wrote a reference letter to the judge; it was not a plea for clemency. In fact, she said, "I do not know anything about Mr. Charles Keating's work or his business or the matters you are dealing with." She explained, "Mr. Keating has done much to help the poor, which is why I am writing to you on his behalf."[32]

The British transplant liked to quote Mother Teresa saying that her congregation has taken a special vow to work for the poor. "This vow," she said, "means that we cannot work for the rich; neither can we accept money for the work we do. Ours has to be a free service, and to the poor."[33] This seems innocent enough, even noble. But to Hitchens, it smacked of dishonesty. He reasons that because she took money from the rich, she was working for them. This is absurd, and surely he knew the difference between soliciting money from the rich and working for them.

[32] Donohue, "Hating Mother Teresa."
[33] Ibid.

There is a larger issue here. If those who seek to help the poor should not take from the rich, whom should they take from? The middle class? Would it make sense to take from the poor, and then give the money back? Doesn't everyone who wants to help the poor — or raise money for any worthy cause — solicit donations from those most in a position to give?

Hitchens was so irrational in his hatred of Mother Teresa that he faulted her for consorting with Hillary Clinton and Prime Minister Margaret Thatcher. To be sure, both of these women have had their fair share of critics, but so what? Why was it improper for Mother Teresa to consort with them? Because Hitchens disdained them?

The Canadian critics not only agree with Hitchens about this; but they also add to the list of persons whom they say are proof of Mother Teresa's agenda. These questionable persons include President Ronald Reagan, Lady Diana, and former New York Mayor Rudy Giuliani. To show how twisted their thinking is, they put these people in the same camp with Fidel Castro.

Navin Chawla is an Indian civil servant who wrote a biography about Mother Teresa. He has a very different understanding of this issue. "It is not in India alone that all doors are open to Mother Teresa. Wherever she finds herself, should she feel the need to call on a city father or the country's chief executive, she is usually received immediately. Everyone knows that she does not go for herself, but for problems concerning the poor, or on account of some difficulties that her Sisters might face."[34]

Moreover, as Chawla describes, while she did not balk at meeting political leaders, she was no partisan. For example, when the U.S. and Iraq went to war, she wrote to the leaders in both nations pleading for peace. The health minister of Iraq was so taken by her plea that he invited the Missionaries of Charity to help the orphaned and the disabled. Chawla emphasizes that the nuns were never in it for themselves.

It is a sad fact that much of the world is run by despots. Given the nature of her work, it was inevitable that Mother Teresa knew many of them. If they allowed her to serve the needy, she did so willingly, yet for this she was, and still is, criticized.

[34] Navin Chawla, *Mother Teresa* (Rockport, MA: Element, 1992), 175.

Consorting with the Rich and Famous

It is undeniably true that Jean-Claude (Baby Doc) Duvalier, and his wife Michèle, oppressed their own people. It is also true that Mother Teresa took money from them. The money, of course, went to the poor. The critics are right to say that the Duvaliers helped to create the poverty, but they are wrong to say that it tainted the work of the nuns. If they did not take the money and spend it on the poor, would the needy have been better off?

Mother Teresa never got involved in the debate over the causes of poverty. That is a matter for intellectuals. What mattered to her was helping the poor. When it came to a nation's leaders, her only goal was to secure their permission to carry out her work.

No one was more severe on this issue than Hitchens. He was perturbed that Mother Teresa did not distinguish between the poor who lived in a democracy and those who did not. He also found fault with her for not distinguishing between right-wing dictatorships (Haiti) and left-wing dictatorships (Albania), as if it mattered to their victims. To Hitchens, this was unforgivable. If his logic made any sense, it would be fair to criticize the Peace Corps and the Red Cross for "courting" despots.

Even more disconcerting is Hitchens' duplicity: he had no principled objection to dictatorships. In 1983, he lamented the "tenth anniversary of the slaughter of Chilean democracy." His hero was Salvador Allende, a corrupt and tyrannical ruler who welcomed terrorists from all over Latin America. Allende not only bankrupted the poor with runaway inflation, but he also locked up dissidents, installed a censorial press, and abused the courts. Hitchens also embraced the Sandinistas in Nicaragua, the left-wing gangsters who plundered their own people.[35]

[35] Donohue, "Hating Mother Teresa."

Chapter 8

Where Did the Money Go?

Not only are Mother Teresa's critics unhappy with some of her donors; they are furious that they don't know exactly how she spent the money. The Canadian writers declare that most of the "bank accounts were kept secret." But are not most bank accounts "kept secret"? Even more bizarre is the fact that on the very next page, where they deplore the "secret" bank accounts, the professors tell us that Chatterjee was able to bust the secret.[36]

---

[36] Larivée, Chénard, and Sénéchal, "The Dark Side of Mother Teresa," 331.

"With the help of the Ministry of Home Affairs in Delhi," they write, "Chatterjee obtained information about MC [Missionaries of Charity] bank accounts throughout India." He found up to $7 million, money derived from numerous prize awards and donors. The professors consider this amount to be "astounding," although anyone who tracks charitable holdings would be unimpressed.[37]

No matter; what bothers them is "Mother Teresa's tight-fisted management." This leads them to "wonder what happened to the millions intended for the poorest of the poor."[38] Since they have no proof of any wrongdoing, this is the best they can do — plant a seed of doubt. They also criticize the nuns for their travel expenses, as if they were partying in Vegas.

Gonzalez is troubled to learn that the nuns "consistently fail to provide statistics on the efficacy of their work."[39] But there is no ready yardstick to measure the success of outreach programs to lepers. And how

[37] Ibid., 332.
[38] Ibid.
[39] "The Humanist Interview with Hemley Gonzalez."

does one measure the efficacy of programs designed to comfort the dying?

Chatterjee is just as hypercritical. His beef? He wants to know how much money was spent on the convents.[40] But why should overhead costs matter to an atheist critic of the nuns? Obviously, there must be enough to house, feed, and clothe the sisters, as well as to cover extraneous expenses. He knows this, but that is not his point: what bothers him is that some of the revenue goes to pay for the welfare of the nuns. Of course, without them, there would be no one to care for the poor.

Chawla tells us that "Mother Teresa has always refused any effort of fundraising. In fact, she specifically forbids it." When donations are received, they go to the regional superior, who decides how the funds should be distributed. "I need money to use for my people," Mother Teresa told him, not for investment purposes. "The quite remarkable sums that are donated are spent almost as quickly on medicines

[40] Dr. Aroup Chatterjee, letter to the editor, *Observer*, December 17, 1995.

(particularly for leprosy and tuberculosis), on food and on milk powder," the superior says.[41]

Here's another fact that Mother Teresa's critics ignore. "The food they eat is not bought with money." They get it from expensive hospitals, chain supermarkets, and from butchers and bakers who give them food they would otherwise discard. Volunteers help with the collection and distribution, and they do so because they want to help the sisters. That's how they make ends meet.[42]

[41] Chawla, *Mother Teresa*, 75.
[42] Ibid., 96.

Chapter 9

Critics Assess the Quality of Care

Early on in her ministry, a sensational story appeared in the Calcutta press about Mother Teresa. A senior nun, Sister Emaques, told reporters horrible stories about ill treatment of the sick, and the "dictatorial" ways of Mother Teresa; the dispirited nun said this is why she left the order. It was all a lie: there was no nun by that name. When Mother Teresa tried to correct the story, sending a letter to the editor, the newspaper refused to print it. She commented, "I feel sorry for those who have written such a story only to sell more papers. How can they misuse our name like that?"[43]

[43] Chawla, *Mother Teresa*, 71.

Unmasking Mother Teresa's Critics

While lies about Mother Teresa's work continue, most of her critics distort her record not by telling intentional falsehoods, but by making serious misjudgments about the nature of her work.

Hitchens often said that "she was not a friend of the poor. She was a friend of *poverty*" (his italics). That's a good line, but the facts are otherwise. She had no means to conquer poverty, but she did have means to treat and comfort the afflicted. To Hitchens, however, she "spent her life opposing the only known cure for poverty, which is the empowerment of women and the emancipation of them from a livestock version of compulsory reproduction."[44]

Even though Hitchens was pro-life, he never allowed this to stand in the way of berating Mother Teresa for condemning abortion. It did not occur to him that if the empowerment he speaks of—allowing women access to abortion—were the enemy of poverty, then China should have little poverty. But its one-child policy (now being revised), which rests

44 Christopher Hitchens, "Mommie Dearest," *Slate*, October 20, 2003, slate.com.

on the principle of compulsory abortion, has neither liberated women nor reduced poverty. Indeed, as a direct result of this barbaric policy, China has the highest rate of female suicide in the world.

Hitchens made millions in America—sometimes in venture capitalist projects—yet his commitment to socialism never wavered. He accurately saw in Mother Teresa someone who would not cooperate with statist policies, but he was not accurate in his assessment of her deeds.

For example, he and the Canadian authors cite Mother Teresa's refusal to put an elevator in a New York City building that she was acquiring to serve the homeless.[45] They interpret this as an example of her willingness to forsake the best interests of the poor for the sake of maintaining an ascetic environment for the nuns. What neither Hitchens nor the Canadians mention is that she and the Missionaries of Charity pledged to carry the handicapped up the stairs.

---

[45] See Donohue, "Hating Mother Teresa," and Larivée, Chénard, and Sénéchal, "The Dark Side of Mother Teresa," 329.

Gonzalez speaks about the lack of a sanitary envi-ronment in the Calcutta homes run by the nuns, and no doubt the settings were often substandard. But when the clients are frequently diseased men and women living in a hospice—persons with no other place to go—keeping the conditions immaculate is a challenge. If this were all he complained about, that would be one thing, but it isn't.

Here's an example of Gonzalez's thinking: "The nuns made us put on a fresh new pair of cotton pants each time [on the patients]. What we needed were diapers or something similar."[46] This is hardly the kind of criticism that should make the alarms go off, but to him it was sufficient. Most telling is his assess-ment of a nun who didn't move as fast as he says she should have.

Gonzalez relates a story about a nun who failed to give a dying man the last rites (never mind that only a priest can offer last rites). He said she was tied up with other patients and did not immediately come

---

[46] Gonzalez, "Dr. Aroup Chatterjee and Hemley Gonzalez Discuss Mother Teresa."

when summoned by him; by the time she came, the man was dead. Not knowing any more about this, it is hard to judge, but it is not hard to assess his judgment of her. "There is real evil inside that human being," he said.[47] If this doesn't discredit him, nothing does.

Chatterjee is just as critical, although not as condemnatory, about the care. He raises questions about the cramped quarters for the sick and the dying. Let's concede his point. Does it not matter that the resources and the number of sisters serving these patients were both limited, making some problems unavoidable? Similarly, his criticism of the sisters for dispensing "inferior powdered milk" to infants is not tempered by the limited options that were available to them.

Putting the nuns under a microscope is one thing, but to misrepresent the accounts of those who observed their work is indefensible. This is what the Canadian authors did: they failed to give an honest assessment of the work of Robin Fox, an American doctor who visited Calcutta.[48]

[47] Ibid.
[48] Larivée, Chénard, and Sénéchal, "The Dark Side of Mother Teresa," 328.

Unmasking Mother Teresa's Critics

While Fox noted some deficiencies in the care of the needy, most of his observations put the sisters in a good light. The Canadian writers, however, give just the opposite impression — they would have the reader believe that Fox hammered the nuns for ill treatment. Here are some comments made by Fox that are nowhere represented by the Canadians. [I will leave the misspelling of Mother Teresa's name intact.]

Speaking of Calcutta, Fox said, "A walk through that squalid part of the city will show you disease and degradation on a grand scale. The fact that the people seldom die on the street is largely thanks to the work of Mother Theresa and her mission." He notes that "if the hospitals refuse admission, Mother Theresa's Home for the Dying will provide."[49]

Fox visited the homes with his wife. "I was surprised to see many of the inmates eating heartily and doing well," he said. "These days, it seems, more than two-thirds leave the home on their feet. Their common feature is not that they were originally perceived

[49] Robin Fox, letter to the editor, *Lancet* 344, September 17, 1994, 807–808.

to be dying but that they had failed to gain admission elsewhere." He admits that the medical care was haphazard—doctors dropped by from time to time—leaving the sisters and volunteers to "make decisions as best they can."[50]

The Canadians say that Fox noted "the deplorable lack of hygiene on the premises, the lack of actual treatment," and so forth.[51] Now match that up with what he really said: "So the most important features of the regimen are cleanliness, the tending of wounds and sores, and loving kindness."[52] The authors are guilty of much more than spin—they are intellectually dishonest.

Finally, Fox has something to say to those who claim that Mother Teresa did not spend donations properly. "If you give money to Mother Theresa's home, don't expect it to be spent on some little luxury."[53]

[50] Ibid.
[51] Larivée, Chénard, and Sénéchal, "The Dark Side of Mother Teresa," 328.
[52] Fox, letter to the editor.
[53] Ibid.

Chapter 10

Honest Accounts of
the Quality of Care

Celeste Owen-Jones volunteered on two occasions, offering her services to the Missionaries of Charity, in Calcutta and in Cuzco. "I have therefore been able to experience firsthand the work these women do as they follow the example set by Mother Teresa," she offered.[54]

Her account takes on even greater significance because of who she is: she is an ex-Catholic who does

---

[54] Celeste Owen-Jones, "A Response to Mother Teresa's Critics," *Huffington Post*, May 7, 2013, huffingtonpost.com.

not believe in saints, miracles, the idea of an after-life, or virtually any of the dogmas of the Church. Yet she proudly defends the yeoman work of Mother Teresa and is highly critical of the accounts rendered by Hitchens and the Canadians.

"Most of the people the sisters care for are physically and mentally handicapped, or very old and very sick," Owen-Jones says. "They live in places where it's hard enough to survive when you are young and healthy. I have seen the sisters do everything they can to make these people's lives better and I have seen their heart ripped apart when a little girl died one morning in Cuzco." She concedes that these patients would receive better care in "an expensive American hospital," but that was never an option. A realist, she says the girl "had a far better life than the one she would have had had the sisters left her in the garbage they found her in."[55]

Speaking of Mother Teresa, Owen-Jones says, "Her fundamental belief is that everyone, absolutely everyone in this world deserves love and care. She

[55] Ibid.

cherished every single life on this planet more than anyone ever did, and that's why she created the Missionaries of Charity: to help and welcome the poorest of the poor, those whose life had not been judged worthy to live and who had been rejected by everything and everyone."[56]

What is it that fired Mother Teresa? What is it that accounts for her incredible commitment to the poor? "Without the belief that every life is worth it and therefore that abortion and contraception are wrong," Owen-Jones writes, "she would not have created such a powerful organization, nor would she have had the strength to carry it on her shoulder all her life." She explains that Mother Teresa's "belief in the sanctity of life was her main driving force to do the good that she did." This assessment carries additional weight because Owen-Jones is an abortion-rights advocate.[57]

Like Owen-Jones, Prabir Ghosh is not a believer. In fact, he is the president of an atheist organization, the Science and Rationalists' Association of India.

[56] Ibid.
[57] Ibid.

Unmasking Mother Teresa's Critics

He does not believe in miracles and even goes so far
as to say that to attribute them to Mother Teresa is
nothing short of "criminal." But he knows of her work
with the sick and the dying and is convinced that on
that count alone she deserves to be named a saint.
"If she is bestowed with sainthood for her service to
mankind," he says, "that will be a great thing."[58]

Vijay Prashad was born and raised in Calcutta. He
is a Communist who is critical of Mother Teresa for
her associations with the rich and famous. But this
doesn't stop him from praising her work.

Prashad credits Mother Teresa for her training as a
medical missionary and particularly for her work with
lepers and children. The Missionaries, he says, "certainly brought relief for many people, not in medical
terms, but with love and affection. Mother Teresa's
Sisters attempted to soothe the ails of the ill and dying
with the balm of love, since many had only rudimen-
tary training in the arts of medicine." He compares
her to Mahatma Gandhi (Indira Gandhi was among

[58] "Scientists Question Cancer Patient's 'Saintly Cure,'"
Post (South Africa), E1 Edition, December 23, 2015, 17.

her admirers), observing that both of them understood that "poverty is the condition of saintliness," and that the poor must be counted among "the blessed."[59]

One of Mother Teresa's biographers, Navin Chawla, said that his work with the Missionaries of Charity "made him a different person." Of Mother Teresa, he says, "She pushed me to be in contact with the poor around me. She was able to touch something in me and has done [so] with hundreds of thousands of people [by] setting a good example."[60]

Chawla speaks admiringly of the many "Co-Workers," or volunteers, who worked with the nuns. Doctors, dentists, nurses—professionals of all kinds —have generously given of their time. He estimates that in Calcutta, Hindu Co-Workers outnumber Christian Co-Workers ten to one. He said that they are not widely known because "they are forbidden to engage in publicity or fund-raising."[61] In his estima-

---

[59] Vijay Prashad, "Mother Teresa: A Communist View," *Australian Marxist Review* 40 (August 1998), cpa.org.au/.

[60] Pentin, "Mother Teresa to Be Canonized."

[61] Chawla, *Mother Teresa*, 97–98.

tion, the homes for children, the dying, and lepers are the crowning achievement of the nuns.

Mother Teresa opened her first children's home, or Shishu Bhavan, in 1955. These homes are not simply residences for premature and sick children; when space is available, kindergarten schools are provided. But most of the children go to the nearest school. "The cost of education, including uniforms and books," Chawla writes, "is entirely met by the Missionaries of Charity." These schools exist in many places, but "Mother Teresa tries especially hard" to establish them "in each of her leprosy centres."[62]

The children brought to these homes are often infants who "are unable to survive premature births, attempted abortions or the aftermath of drug abuse by expectant mothers."

Some people have asked the nuns, why bother with them? They are going to die anyway. Mother Teresa answered this with indignation. "I don't understand this. For me, even if a child dies within minutes, that child must not be allowed to die alone and

[62] Ibid., 117–118.

uncared for." She was often quoted as saying, "If there is an unwanted baby, don't let it die. Send it to me."[63] Spoken like a true saint.

The babies the sisters acquired, or found, were not healthy. Said one nun, "These are usually severely physically and mentally handicapped."[64] Fortunately, many are adopted, even by high-caste Hindu families. "According to Hindu law," explained Mother Teresa, "an adopted child becomes a legal heir and can inherit property."[65]

As Spink recounts, homeless children "were found in garbage cans and drains. Others were simply abandoned on the city railway platforms. Nearly all were suffering from acute malnutrition and tuberculosis; all were crying out for love." The sisters did not find all of the children. "Gradually the word spread — children were sent to Shishu Bhavan by the police, by social workers, by doctors, and eventually by hospitals."[66]

[63] Ibid., 119–120.
[64] Ibid., 119.
[65] Ibid., 124.
[66] Spink, *Mother Teresa*, 58–59.

The children were badly damaged. "Some of the babies were so tiny that the prospect of their survival was minimal; some of the older children, with emaciated limbs, distended stomachs and eyes that seemed prematurely old, were permanently scarred by their experiences. No child was ever refused a home, however, even if it meant that the babies slept there three or more to a cot or were coaxed into life in a box heated by a light bulb."[67]

The boys and girls are offered services appropriate to their situation. If a boy is too old for adoption, he is sent to the Boys' Homes, run by the Missionary Brothers of Charity, a branch of the order. Girls who do not possess the academic qualities necessary to find a husband are given a small dowry, without which they would likely have to remain single. "There are innumerable girls" from these homes who are now "well settled," Chawla says, "with happy families of their own."[68]

The Homes for the Dying were established by Mother Teresa out of necessity: hospitals often refused

[67] Ibid., 59.
[68] Chawla, *Mother Teresa*, 120–121.

to accept those who appeared to be deathly ill. Contrary to what her critics allege, the nuns did not simply give them love; they did everything they could to help them recover.

Chawla notes that in the 1940s and 1950s, "nearly all those who were admitted succumbed to illnesses. In the 1960s and 1970s, the mortality rate was roughly half those admitted. In the last ten years or so [meaning the 1980s to the early 1990s], only a fifth died."[69] So much for the myth that the sisters never tried to acquire medicinal help.

Mother Teresa could never do this alone and was always proud to speak about her volunteers. "They come from all over the world. They work [in their respective countries] to earn money, and then they come here to serve others. They, themselves, pay for everything, because we give them nothing." As Chawla details, these volunteers are "constantly on their hands and knees scrubbing the floors, changing bed clothes, mopping urine-soaked beds, feeding or

[69] Ibid., 163.

holding sick people," and the like.[70] And they come from all over for this because of one person, Mother Teresa.

The care shown for lepers is another classic example of Mother Teresa's vocation. Chawla notes that most nations in the developed world have at least one leprosy station, and in some countries there are several. Mother Teresa typically set them up outside city limits, and that is because of resistance from urban officials; she also did not want to encourage the afflicted to beg in the streets.[71] The stigma attached to those suffering from leprosy is one more hurdle that Mother Teresa constantly fought.

The leper asylums cost a lot of money to build and maintain, but that was never a problem. For instance, in 1965, Pope Paul VI gave Mother Teresa the Lincoln Continental limousine he used while visiting India. She thanked him and then raffled it off, using the funds to build a hospital for lepers. Similarly, in the 1970s, when Pope Paul VI gave her a big check,

[70] Ibid., 167.
[71] Ibid., 149.

she spent the money on leper settlements; she did the same with the proceeds from the Joseph P. Kennedy Foundation.[72]

Mother Teresa did not forget modern-day lepers, those dying of AIDS. In the 1980s, she founded New York's first AIDS hospice in Greenwich Village. Moreover, she successfully pushed for the release of three prisoners from Sing Sing who were suffering from AIDS; they were given a new home in the Village.

New York City Mayor Ed Koch was blown away by her kindness. "She said that when AIDS patients were near death, she would sit at their bedside. Often they would take her hands and place her fingers on their faces wanting her to feel their lesions and to close their eyelids for the last time." Mother Teresa said about this experience, "They were asking for a ticket to heaven, and I gave them that ticket."[73]

[72] Spink, *Mother Teresa*, 160.
[73] Ed Koch, "A Saint for All Seasons," *New York Post*, undated essay.

Chapter 11

Mother Teresa
Confounds Her Critics

Students in the social sciences are taught that if they want to understand how others think, they need to adopt what sociologist Max Weber called *Verstehen*, or sympathetic understanding; they need to try to see the world through the lens of their subject.

Regrettably, when it comes to the critics of Mother Teresa, they express no interest in judging her work from a Catholic perspective. That is because so many of them are highly critical of Catholicism, if not downright disdainful of it. To cite one prominent example, they are not so much ignorant of what Catholics call redemptive suffering; they are contemptuous of it.

Redemptive suffering is the conviction that we can unite with God by surrendering our sufferings to Christ. Historian James Hitchcock perceptively notes that "this is an extremely radical concept. Neither before or after Christ has any religion interpreted pain and suffering this way."[74] That's because no other religion sees the Cross as the means of salvation.

Those who assess the record of Mother Teresa without appreciating the centrality that redemptive suffering played in her work cannot fully understand who she was. "We are all called to be saints," she wrote. "Don't be afraid. There must be the cross, there must be suffering, a clear sign that Jesus has drawn you so close to His heart that He can share His suffering with you."[75] It was for this reason that she told President Reagan, after he was shot, that his suffering would bring him closer to Jesus.[76]

---

[74] Donohue, *The Catholic Advantage*, 67.

[75] Ibid., 78–79.

[76] Spink, *Mother Teresa*, 184.

"Suffering in itself is nothing," she said, "but suffering with Christ's passion is a wonderful gift. Man's most beautiful gift is that he can share in the passion of Christ."[77]

No one, of course, is obliged to agree with Mother Teresa, but if those who seek to evaluate her work don't understand how important the concept of redemptive suffering was to her, they can never figure her out. That is their fault, not hers.

Those who see redemptive suffering as a dark vision, or as a sign of resignation, fail to capture its essence. "Remember that the passion of Christ ends always in the joy of the resurrection of Christ," Mother Teresa said, "so when you feel in your own heart the suffering of Christ, remember that the resurrection has to come."[78] In other words, the sorrow of Good Friday is followed by the joy of Easter.

Hitchens never appreciated this defining Catholic belief. A militant atheist, he could never comprehend how Mother Teresa could console the terminally ill

[77] Ibid., 144.
[78] Donohue, *The Catholic Advantage*, 73.

by saying, "You are suffering like Christ on the cross. So Jesus must be kissing you."[79]

Hitchens notwithstanding, Mother Teresa did not spend her days in prayer asking God to grow the ranks of the destitute; she spent her days in prayer, and service, so that the destitute could experience hope. That was something he could not grasp. Furthermore, his disdain for the concept of redemptive suffering is easy to understand: he believed in neither Christ nor redemption.

Hitchens was not alone in mocking Mother Teresa's belief in redemptive suffering. Chatterjee accused her of having a "warped mentality,"[80] and Kempton said that she adopted this stance for "the primary purpose of affording the comfortable a chance to discover how virtuous they are."[81]

Interestingly, if someone were to say that many Native American traditions are primitive, and are indeed proof of Native Americans' "warped mentality,"

[79] Donohue, "Hating Mother Teresa."
[80] Gonzalez, "Dr. Aroup Chatterjee and Hemley Gonzalez Discuss Mother Teresa."
[81] Kempton, "The Shadow Saint."

he would be branded a bigot, especially by people like Chatterjee. As for Kempton, if he thinks for a moment that Mother Teresa lived a comfortable existence, or that she congratulated herself for being so noble, it only proves his ignorance. Nothing could be further from the truth.

The Canadian professors offer more of the same. According to their understanding of redemptive suffering, if God loves the poor, and their suffering brings them closer to Him, this means that "keeping misery alive" is a plus.[82]

Although it is beyond the comprehension of those who cannot appreciate the meaning of redemptive suffering, no practicing Catholic believes that because our sufferings unite us with Christ, the more, the merrier. Only cynical professors are capable of reaching such a conclusion.

Mother Teresa was slammed by all of these critics for setting up hospices, instead of hospitals. In her defense, Father James Martin notes that "primary

---

[82] Larivée, Chénard, and Sénéchal, "The Dark Side of Mother Teresa," 330.

care is not what Mother Teresa's order was founded to do. There are hundreds of Catholic medical orders which generously fill that need.... Rather, the charism of the Missionaries of Charity (with whom I have worked) is, quite specifically, to provide solace to the very many poor patients who would otherwise die alone."[83]

Father Peter Gumpel told Bill Doino the same thing. Mother Teresa and her sisters filled the gap that hospitals left. "What many do not understand is the desperate conditions Mother Teresa constantly faced, and that her special charism was not to found or run hospitals ... but to rescue those who were given no chance of surviving, and otherwise would have died in the street."[84]

To criticize someone for not achieving what he never set out to do is simply absurd. Worse, to disparage those who comfort the sick and dying in their last days is downright cruel. If it mattered to their

---

[83] Father James Martin, letter to the editor, *New York Review of Books*, September 19, 1996.

[84] Doino, "Mother Teresa and Her Critics."

patients—and it did—why shouldn't that count? Indeed, why shouldn't that count above all else?

Gonzalez is troubled to learn that Mother Teresa and her sisters did not see themselves as social workers. This bothers him so much that he actually questions their motives for tending to the poor. A materialist, he thinks that helping the poor is a secular vocation, one that requires training, preferably in a school of social work. In fairness, there is much to applaud about the profession of social work, but there is no academic institution that can teach us how to love the poor, and that was Mother Teresa's special gift. To learn that, we need to set our sights higher.

Kathryn Spink's splendid biography of Mother Teresa recounts how government workers in New Delhi once asked her to train their social workers. They wanted to know her secret; they thought it was the result of some new sociological insight. Spink relates why she had to decline their request.

Whatever good the sisters were able to do, Spink says, "was entirely dependent on the recognition of Christ in the poor and on spiritual values to which social work, very good and commendable though it might be, gave insufficient credence." Furthermore, she says, "without the purity of heart vital to the seeing of God, without the framework and grounding of the religious life, Mother Teresa was firmly convinced that her sisters would be unable to bring peace to the dying, touch the open wounds of the leper, and nurture the tiny spark of life in babies whom others had abandoned."[85] There is no state-run program, in any nation, that is capable of doing that.

Similarly, when Prime Minister Thatcher boasted to Mother Teresa that Britain had a fine welfare system, the saintly nun replied, "But do you have love?"[86] For Mother Teresa, helping the poor is ideally a personal exchange, an ongoing relationship between the two parties; it is not a "program." This is a quintessentially Catholic idea, something that baffles many atheists and socialists.

Simon Leys captures the essence of Mother Teresa's greatness. His reply to those who say that the nuns failed to provide adequate living quarters for the

[85] Spink, *Mother Teresa*, 70–71.
[86] Pentin, "Mother Teresa to Be Canonized."

sick and the dying is worth repeating. "When I am on my death bed," he wrote, "I think I should prefer to have one of her Sisters by my side, rather than a modern social worker."[87]

[87] Leys, letter to the editor.

Chapter 12

Deriding Her
Lifestyle and Beliefs

When Pope Paul VI heard of her work, Mother Teresa was called to Rome in 1963. A monsignor told her to change her clothes, objecting to her white sari; he asked that she put on a traditional black outfit before she met the pope. She replied, "These clothes are good enough for God."[88]

The poor monsignor meant well, but he didn't get it: Mother Teresa chose an ascetic lifestyle, and she did so because it allowed her to identify with the less

[88] "Mother Teresa," *All Things Considered*, National Public Radio, September 5, 1997.

fortunate. To say that her critics find this idea deplorable would be an understatement.

Hitchens objected to her asceticism, saying that it stemmed from Jesus' comment that "the poor will always be with you" (cf. Matt. 26:11). Not surprisingly, Hitchens said, "I remember as a child finding this famous crack rather unsatisfactory. Either one eschews luxury and serves the poor or one does not."[89]

He did not understand that while Mother Teresa eschewed luxury and served the poor, not for a minute did she think she was conquering poverty. His own lifestyle also made it hard for him to appreciate her asceticism: he was promiscuous with men, women, alcohol, and cigarettes.

Some of those unhappy with the austere lifestyle of Mother Teresa are given to bizarre commentary. Take author Krishna Dutta. A native of Calcutta, she wrote a book about its cultural and literary history. Speaking of Mother Teresa, she said, "She hardly connected herself with the city she lived in for more than six decades — and completely neglected its cultural and

---

[89] Donohue, "Hating Mother Teresa."

intellectual life."[90] True enough. It was certainly true of Jesus as well. Perhaps they had better things to do—such as serving outcasts.

When Mother Teresa died, an American reporter described the way she lived, without the familiar derision. "Like her nuns," she wrote, "Mother Teresa lived simply. They own only three saris, sleep on thin mattresses, wash their clothes by hand and sit on chapel floors."[91] As Chawla reports, she even refused a washing machine. "There is no television, video, fax machine, even an oven or a toaster. In the kitchen, the food continues to be cooked on a charcoal fire, the fuel of the very poor."[92]

Why? Why did she live this way? Her answer is something that all her critics should ponder. "We do not want to do what other religious orders have done throughout history," she said, "and begin by serving the poor only to end up unconsciously serving the rich. In order to understand and help those who have

[90] Dutta, "Saint of the Gutter with Friends in High Places."
[91] Lori Sham, "Mother Teresa's Heart Never Left the Poor," *USA Today*, September 8, 1997, 17A.
[92] Chawla, *Mother Teresa*, 69–70.

nothing, we must live like them.... The only difference is that these people are poor by birth, and we are poor by choice."[93] Surely one does not have to be Catholic to understand this.

Catholics put a premium on forgiveness—it is one of their most valued and conspicuous attributes—and few embodied this virtue more than Mother Teresa. But to her critics, her willingness to forgive was a problem. So when she forgave those responsible for the Union Carbide explosion that erupted in Bhopal in 1984, killing thousands, she was faulted for doing so. Hitchens ripped her for appearing apologetic, and condemned the capitalists for causing the explosion.[94] More recently, the Canadian professors slammed her as well.[95]

Never mind that the Indian government was mostly to blame, the idea that Mother Teresa was giving cover to greedy capitalists is nonsense. Indeed, it is the kind of conjecture we would expect from critics

[93] Ibid., 44.
[94] Donohue, "Hating Mother Teresa."
[95] Larivée, Chénard, and Sénéchal, "The Dark Side of Mother Teresa," 330.

who have no evidence to support their claims. If they had any appreciation for how consistent she was—she always offered forgiveness to those who caused great harm—they might not make such a scurrilous charge.

The Canadians take this a step further. They fault her and the sisters for spending so much time praying for the victims of natural disasters and for baptizing the sick and the dying. So what should the nuns have done? They suggest that it would have made more sense to engage in "direct intervention."[96] Evidently, the professors have yet to learn that the Missionaries of Charity take their cues from Jesus, not Saul Alinsky.

Simon Leys gets it right again. "The material act of baptism consists in shedding a few drops of water on the head of a person, while mumbling a dozen simple ritual words. Either you believe in the supernatural effect of this gesture—and then you should dearly wish for it. Or you do not believe in it, and the gesture is as innocent and well-meaningly innocuous as chasing a fly away with a wave of the hand."

[96] Ibid., 228–230.

He offers an interesting analogy. "If a cannibal who happens to love you presents you with his most cherished possession—a magic crocodile tooth that should protect you forever—will you indignantly reject his gift for being primitive and superstitious, or would you gratefully accept it as a generous mark of sincere concern and affection?"

He concludes, that "Jesus was spat upon—not by journalists, as there were none in His time. It is now Mother Teresa's privilege to experience this particular updating of her Master's predicament."[97]

There are plenty of atheists who admire the work of these nuns, and even appreciate the sincerity of their beliefs. Unfortunately, this is not true of the atheists who are obsessed with Mother Teresa.

[97] Leys, letter to the editor.

Chapter 13

Mother Teresa's "Dark Nights"

In the late summer of 2007, *Time* magazine ran a story by David Van Biema that shook the Catholic world, and beyond. Did Mother Teresa lose her faith in Jesus?[98]

The article was written in the wake of a book that was edited by Mother Teresa's advocate for sainthood, Father Brian Kolodiejchuk, titled, *Come Be My Light: The Private Writings of the "Saint of Calcutta."* The volume was a collection of letters that were exchanged between Mother Teresa and her confessors

[98] David Van Biema, "Mother Teresa's Crisis of Faith," *Time*, August 23, 2007.

and superiors, spanning six and a half decades. They reveal that for almost half a century, she did not feel God's presence in either her heart or in the Eucharist.

Immediately, her critics expressed their delight: They now possessed irrefutable evidence that even Mother Teresa did not believe in God.

Before addressing the particulars, one might have thought that her critics would have at least moved cautiously when the news broke. After all, the letters were not published by an investigative reporter for the *New York Times*, or some *60 Minutes* producer. It was the "secretive" Vatican that authorized these revelations.

Moreover, it was her own man—the priest who championed her cause—who published the letters; they were discovered in 2003 during the probe into her candidacy for sainthood. Why would he want to undercut his efforts and work against her? It soon became plain that her critics jumped the gun, misinterpreting what she said.

The letters are poignant. We learn that less than three months before she won the Nobel Prize in 1979, Mother Teresa wrote to her spiritual confidant, Father

Michael van der Peet, saying that she no longer felt the presence of Jesus in her life. She confessed that "the silence and the emptiness is so great, that I look and do not see—Listen and do not hear—the tongue moves [in prayer] but does not speak."[99]

What happened to Mother Teresa is not unprecedented. "Dark nights," or great periods of doubt, have gripped many saints, including St. John of the Cross, St. Thérèse of Lisieux, and St. Paul of the Cross. To be sure, these are heartbreaking experiences, but as Father Gumpel notes, "persevering and overcoming" these dark chapters "is considered one of the signs of sanctity."[100]

What does this tell us about Mother Teresa? The late Father Richard McBrien, long-time theologian at the University of Notre Dame, expressed it well. "It shows that she wasn't a plaster-of-Paris saint who never had a doubt about God or the ultimate meaning of life. This can only enhance her reputation as a saintly person with people who aren't easily impressed

[99] Ibid.
[100] Doino, "Mother Teresa and Her Critics."

with pious stories." And what about her detractors? "Those who think otherwise have a lot of learning to do about the complexities of life and about the nature of faith."[101]

There are some, like her Canadian critics, who are not interested in learning about life's complexities and the nature of faith. They are more interested in promoting the idea that Mother Teresa's periods of doubt suggest just how insane she was.

To make this claim, they cite Father Kolodiejchuk's observation that the "dark nights" of suffering that Mother Teresa endured allowed her to relive Christ's agony on the Cross. The Canadian professors, citing the work of others, say this is a reflection of her poor mental health, a condition they say is related to schizophrenia.[102]

If that were true, it would mean that every Catholic who believes in redemptive suffering is at least

---

[101] Eric Gorski, "New Book Showing Mother Teresa's Faith Struggle Prompts a Reexamination of Her Legacy," *Associated Press*, August 25, 2007.

[102] Larivée, Chénard, and Sénéchal, "The Dark Side of Mother Teresa," 334.

borderline crazy. Given that there are well over a billion Catholics in the world, that's a pretty big problem. Or it may mean, as I have often said, that there is not much difference between the academy and the asylum.

The Canadian authors cannot resist the temptation to psychoanalyze Mother Teresa. She was "depressed." She never got over the "death of her father." Her "pain, anger, fear and confusion" stemmed from her "spiritual life." Most of all, her embrace of God was a consequence of her need for a paternal figure; it was not a sincere vocational experience.[103]

The problem with this game — and in the hands of an ideologue, psychoanalysis can quickly descend to the level of a game — is that anyone can play. No training is needed; no evidence is required; no data must be presented; no proof of any kind will be summoned. Conjecture is all that counts.

For example, it could be contended that her Canadian critics are working through a traumatic event in their lives: they are suffering from God envy, a

[103] Ibid., 335.

deep-seated inability to connect with anyone but themselves; they also have a pathological fear of the transcendent. Thus, they lash out at people of faith, especially religious notables who make them feel inadequate. Is this true? Who knows? But it is just as persuasive as their psychoanalysis of Mother Teresa, although they would be aghast at the comparison.

No one is better situated to evaluate Mother Teresa's predicament than Father Kolodiejchuk. He knew her for twenty years and collected all the documents that were submitted to validate her candidacy for sainthood. He regrets that *Time* twisted the meaning of his book. He explains that the title of the book, *Come Be My Light*, comes from "the words Jesus spoke to Mother Teresa in 1947." To be specific, "in 1942," he says, "Mother vowed to never deny Jesus anything. It was soon afterwards when she heard Jesus say to her: 'Come, be my light.' "[104] She clearly brought that light to the dispossessed in India.

[104]"Author of New Mother Teresa Book Responds to Time Magazine Article," Catholic News Agency, September 13, 2007.

His central point is conveniently ignored by her critics. "The book is about a trial of faith that Mother endured for 50 years, which is very different from a crisis of faith." The difference is huge. Quite frankly, it is not easy to overcome a crisis of faith, but a trial is different: it is something she was able to overcome by showing that the love "is in the will and not in feelings."[105]

Not unexpectedly, Hitchens seized on the *Time* story, declaring that Mother Teresa "was no more exempt from the realization that religion is a human fabrication."[106] Not only is this wrong; it can easily be disproven. So why would a learned man make such a statement?

On August 28, 2007, I debated Hitchens on this issue on the MSNBC show *Hardball*. He argued that "Mother Teresa did not believe that Jesus was present in the Eucharist." I replied that he didn't make

---

[105] Ibid.

[106] William Donohue, "Mother Teresa's Faith: Hitchens Still Doesn't Get It," *Catalyst*, October 2007, available online at catholicleague.org.

the crucial distinction between feelings and beliefs.[107] Even the *Time* article reported that for decades she "*felt* no presence of God whatsoever" (my italics).[108] Yes, she did not *feel* God's presence in the Eucharist, but she never stopped *believing* in the Real Presence.

To see how utterly wrong Hitchens was, consider what a senior sister of the Missionaries of Charity said about Mother Teresa; it is found in the same book (edited by Father Kolodiejchuk) that the English atheist cites as proof of his position.

> Mother received Holy Communion with tremendous devotion. If there happened to be a second Mass celebrated in [the] Mother House on a given day, she would always try to assist at it, even if she were very busy. I would hear her say on such occasions, "How beautiful to have received Jesus twice today." Mother's deep, deep reverence for the Blessed Sacrament was a sign of her profound faith in the Real Presence of Jesus under the appearance of bread and wine.

[107] Ibid.
[108] Van Biema, "Mother Teresa's Crisis of Faith."

Her adoring attitude, gestures such as genuflections—even on both knees in the presence of the Blessed Sacrament exposed, and that well into old age—her postures such as kneeling and joining hands, her preference for receiving Holy Communion on the tongue all bespoke her faith in the Eucharist.[109]

After the debate with Hitchens, I wrote to Father Kolodiejchuk, asking him to comment on our exchange. He agreed with my comment to Hitchens that "there is a profound difference between 'feeling' and 'believing.'" He then offered his own observation of my remark. "This is the key point which people must come to realize, especially nowadays when the tendency is to reduce the living of our Faith to feelings."[110]

"Though Mother Teresa did not *feel* Jesus' presence in the Eucharist," he wrote, "her firm belief in the

[109]Donohue, "Mother Teresa's Faith."

[110]I called Fr. Kolodiejchuk after the debate with Hitchens, but he was traveling; one of the nuns confirmed that my account was accurate. His letter to me is dated May 26, 2008; it is the source of the quote.

Real Presence cannot be questioned for we have ample confirmation of it by what she said and did: her numerous references to the Eucharist in her speeches, letters and instructions, the way she assisted at Mass, the way she exposed and reposed the Blessed Sacrament for daily Holy Hour, her intense prayer during Adoration, and the way she genuflected and taught her sisters to genuflect as a deliberate act of acknowledging God's Presence in the Tabernacle"[111] (his emphasis).

He also cited the reflections of the Archbishop of Calcutta. The archbishop never forgot what happened when he presided at a Mass attended by Mother Teresa. "It was here for the first time I realized how intense, how fervent, was Mother Teresa's passion for the Sacrament. I watched fascinated as her eyes followed the Eucharist with an almost hungry longing. When she knelt to receive it, she might have been kneeling at the feet of the Lord, there was such ecstasy on her face."[112]

These observations, when coupled with her own admissions about the centrality of the Eucharist in

[111]Kolodiejchuk to Donohue, May 26, 2008.
[112]Ibid.

her life, prove how fatuous Hitchens's remarks are. I knew when I debated him that he was projecting his own lack of faith onto her, which is why I related the following story to him.

I told Hitchens about an encounter Mother Teresa had with a professor in the United States. He asked her if she was married. "Mother Teresa said yes. I am married to a spouse who sometimes makes it difficult for me to smile. His name is Jesus. And that's because he is very demanding."[113]

Louis Armstrong was once asked, "What is jazz?" His reply was brilliant, and it sheds great light on those who cannot understand Mother Teresa. "If you gotta ask," he said, "then you just don't know."

[113]Our MSNBC-TV debate was on *Hardball*, August 28, 2007.

Chapter 14

Assessing Her Miracles

Customarily, the Vatican must approve two miracles before a candidate for sainthood can be canonized; exceptions can be made. Mother Teresa's sainthood journey started when she was beatified in 2003: the Vatican concluded that an Indian woman's tumor was healed as a result of a miracle attributed to her.

The second miracle happened in 2008, although it was not brought to the attention of the postulation committee until the end of 2013. A Brazilian man who suffered from a viral brain disease nearly died; years later his recovery was credited to Mother Teresa's intercession.

Most atheists do not believe in God, miracles, or an afterlife (but some do), so it was to be expected that Mother Teresa's critics would reject both miracles. They did. It was the first miracle, however, that really sent them reeling. Before examining their objections, the second miracle deserves our attention.

The Brazilian man had a brain tumor with multiple abscesses, leaving him in a coma. He was treated by physicians but did not respond. His wife had been praying for months to Mother Teresa, and when he was taken into emergency surgery, she, along with her husband's priest and relatives, prayed all the harder.

He was taken into surgery at 6:10 p.m. on December 9, 2008, and thirty minutes later the neurosurgeon returned to the operating room and inexplicably found him awake and without pain. He asked the doctor, "What am I doing here?"[114]

The next morning he was examined, and the pain was gone; his thinking processes were fine. He was

---

[114]"Mother Teresa to Be Saint as Miracle Approved," *Today*, December 18, 2015, today.ng/news.

told he did not need surgery and was released. Completely healed, he went back to work as a mechanical engineer.

His doctors told him that there was one side effect he could not avoid: he was declared sterile because of his weakened immune system and all the antibiotics that he ingested. They were wrong. In 2009 and 2012, his wife gave birth to two healthy children.[115]

On September 10, 2015, Father Kolodiejchuk reports, a medical commission "voted unanimously that the cure is inexplicable in the light of the present-day medical knowledge." A month later, a theological investigation "voted unanimously that there is a perfect connection between cause and effect between the invocation of Mother Teresa and the scientifically inexplicable healing."[116] Formal approval of the second miracle was given in December 2015.

It was the declaration of the first miracle that proved to be the most contentious.

---

[115]Sewall Chan, "Francis Moves Mother Teresa Closer to Sainthood," *New York Times*, December 19, 2015.
[116]Ibid.

Unmasking Mother Teresa's Critics

In 1998, Monica Besra was living with her husband and five children in a mud-brick house without running water or electricity in the Indian countryside, four hundred miles from Calcutta. They were so poor that they had to take their children out of school to pay down their debts. Feeling ill, Monica was seen by doctors and was diagnosed with a tumor in her abdomen. Out of desperation she sought out the Missionaries of Charity.

The bulge in her stomach was huge and growing. Her tuberculosis was so bad that she was deemed too weak for surgery. The nuns took matters into their own hands and placed a medallion of Mother Teresa (given to them by Mother Teresa) on Monica's abdomen. She fell asleep, and when she awoke the tumor was gone. This miracle took place on September 5, 1998, the first anniversary of the death of Mother Teresa.

Monica's husband, Seiku, did not agree that it was a miracle that healed his wife. "It's much ado about nothing," he said. "My wife was cured by doctors and not by any miracle."[117] One of those doctors, Dr. Ran-

[117]"What's Mother Teresa Got to Do with It?", *Time*, October 13, 2002.

jan Mustafi, agrees, and says it was his treatment that made the difference.[118]

But Monica maintains that it was not the doctors who saved her. Although she previously never believed in miracles, she attributed her recovery wholly to Mother Teresa. In December 2015, she told an English reporter, "When I looked at Mother's picture, I saw rays of white light coming from her eyes. Then I fell unconscious. When I awoke the next morning, the lump was gone."[119]

Mother Teresa's atheist critics, of course, say Monica is delusional. Hitchens quickly cited Dr. Mustafi's claims as proof that no miracle occurred.[120] Prabir Ghosh, the head of the Indian rationalist group, went even further, demanding the arrest of Sister Nirmala, Mother Teresa's successor.

Ghosh issued a formal charge, asking the police to arrest the nun for committing fraud; he accused her

[118]David Rohde, "Her Legacy: Acceptance and Doubts of a Miracle," *New York Times*, October 20, 2003.

[119]Ann Neumann, "The Patient Body: Healthcare and the Kiss of Jesus," The Revealer, January 25, 2016, therevealer.org.

[120]Hitchens, "Mommie Dearest."

of making up stories about the miracle in order to secure sainthood for Mother Teresa.[121] As expected, his efforts went nowhere. But it says a lot about the insecurity of professional atheists — just the belief in miracles is too much for them to tolerate.

An American atheist, Hemant Mehta, is just as apoplectic. He sounded the alarms in a video. "If people genuinely believe she was cured by a miracle," he said, "they may stop taking their medicine, their drugs, whatever will actually help them get better, because they're just waiting for Mother Teresa to intervene."[122]

Mehta cited not a single instance to validate his statement. Ironically, he has it all backward: it is much easier to make the case that those who don't believe in miracles are the most likely to stop treatment that is not working. What do they have to fall back on?

[121] "Indian Rationalists Call Mother Teresa's Miracle Hocus-Pocus," The Naked Truth, May 18, 2015, nakedtruth786. wordpress.com.

[122] Hemant Mehta's video can be found by accessing " 'Friendly Atheist' Video on Why Mother Teresa Shouldn't Be a Saint," World Religion News, May 2, 2016.

Mehta also said that the so-called miracle was a bust, claiming that "Besra suffered for years after Mother Teresa died."[123] Really? In December 2015, just before Christmas, she said, "It's all for Mother that I am living a healthy and happy life. My life would be fulfilled if I can attend her sainthood ceremony."[124]

These atheists have no idea how thorough the investigations are into alleged miracles. Not only that: the researchers work hard to find evidence that would *dispute* claims of a miracle. In the case of Monica, an Episcopal bishop, Salvatore Lobo, said at the time of her recovery that it met all the requirements to be declared a miracle. "It is organic, permanent, immediate and antirecessionary in nature," he said.[125]

Monica's doctors confirmed to reporters at the time that her tumor was the size of a seven-month-old fetus. But when she woke up after the sisters prayed for her, with the medallion of Mother Teresa

[123] Ibid.

[124] "Mother Teresa Has Been Like a God to Me," *Economic Times*, December 21, 2015.

[125] Tessa Berenson, "This Was Mother Teresa's First Miracle," *Time*, December 18, 2015, time.com.

on her stomach, it was gone. "When I got up, at 1:00 in the morning," she said, "I found the big tumor disappeared."[126]

Her physician, Dr. R. N. Bhattacharya, told his side of the story, and it is persuasive. "Medically, OK, I'm a man of medical science," he said. "But to me, I did not find any other reason that without any operation, the tumor of such size would disappear overnight or within two or three days there would be complete recovery."[127]

A CNN correspondent in New Delhi commented that the doctor "has been practicing medicine for 26 years. He's convinced what he saw was a miracle." He admitted that "this is one of the very wonderful experiences I ever had in my medical career."[128]

So who are we to believe? The patient and her attending physician, or the atheist critics of Mother Teresa? Moreover, if a person categorically denies the

[126]Kyra Phillips and Satinder Bindra, "Mother Teresa a Step Closer to Beatification," CNN (live on location), October 1, 2002.
[127]Ibid.
[128]Ibid.

existence of miracles, then nothing can ever dissuade him. This doesn't disprove claims of a miracle; all it proves is that atheists refuse to believe in them.

Chapter 15

Awards and Honors

A medical center in the Philippines is named after Mother Teresa, as are countless schools, streets, and museums throughout the world. When she died, the Missionaries of Charity numbered 4,000; today there are 4,500 religious sisters. They run hospices, clinics, food pantries, counseling programs, orphanages, and schools. It all started in the mid-twentieth century.

Mother Teresa received an unprecedented number of awards and honors. They came from many nations, universities, and religious institutions, spanning several faiths, but there is one accolade she was denied: on the anniversary of her centenary, August 26, 2010, the tower of the Empire State Building did not shine blue and white, as requested. I made the request, and it was turned down by the building's owner, Anthony Malkin.

Malkin is a wealthy real-estate operator who has much in common with Mother Teresa's critics: he supports left-wing causes and is a militant secularist. That is why he denied a request to honor the U.S. Marines but had no problem paying tribute to Mao Zedong: the tower lit up the sky in red in honor of the Chinese Communist who killed seventy-seven million of his own people. But Malkin didn't have the last word on this matter.

I held a rally that night outside the Empire State Building; three thousand turned out in support of Mother Teresa. Speaking at the event were Republicans and Democrats, and people of all races and ethnic groups. Catholic, Protestant, Jewish, Muslim, and Hindu speakers were there, and none held back in denouncing the decision to stiff Mother Teresa. Malkin owned the building, but we owned the day — the public was on our side, and Malkin knew it.[129]

[129]William Donohue, "Understanding Anthony Malkin," *Catalyst*, July/August 2010; see also "Rally Succeeds,"

Mother Teresa is heralded the world over, but this episode only goes to show that for some — diehard radicals and atheists — recognizing the altruistic achievements of a humble Catholic nun is off limits.

The Empire State Building controversy was a media splash, but it was nothing when compared with what happened on the occasion of her most celebrated award, the Nobel Peace Prize; it is still a source of great consternation.

When she won the Nobel Peace Prize in 1979, Mother Teresa took the opportunity to tell the world who the greatest victims of violence are — the unborn. She pointedly said that "the greatest destroyer of peace is abortion." She explained her position with precision. "Because if a mother can kill her own child — what is left for me to kill you and you to kill me — there is nothing between."[130]

Consistent with everything she ever said and did, she once again exclaimed, "The poor people are very

---

Catalyst, October 2010. Both are available online at catholicleague.org.

[130]Mother Teresa's Nobel lecture, December 11, 1979, http://www.nobelprize.org/.

great people," maintaining that "they can teach us so many beautiful things."

She related how one evening she and her sisters picked up four people from the street. She asked the sisters to take care of three of them; she took ownership of the one who was suffering the most. "I put her to bed, and there was such a beautiful smile on her face. She took hold of my hand, as she said one word only: Thank you — and she died."[131]

She also noted that "today there is so much suffering — and I feel that the passion of Christ is being relived all over again — we are there to share that passion, to share that suffering of people." She stressed that in the developing world, the suffering is of a material kind, but in the developed world, suffering means being shut out, unwanted, and unloved.[132]

These are heterodox views, not the kind that most of us are used to hearing. Not surprisingly, the reception was incredible the world over, but to her familiar critics, it was another opportunity to pounce.

[131] Ibid.
[132] Ibid.

Hitchens said it was "strange" that someone who had never advanced the cause of peace would be awarded the Nobel Peace Prize.[133] Similarly, the Canadians found it "strange" that she would cite abortion as the greatest enemy of peace.[134]

These protestations notwithstanding, both knew that she touched a chord when she said that "if a mother can kill her own child," then all bets are off. Surely killing strangers, and those on the battlefield, is easier than killing our own. It makes perfect sense, then, to decry the consequences of becoming inured to the death of unborn children. It is telling that her critics offered no rejoinder, only expressions of dismay.

When she received the Nobel Peace Prize, she requested that the money that had been set aside for the traditional banquet, $192,000, be spent instead on the poor in India. It was vintage Mother Teresa.

At the end of the last century, Gallup did a survey of the most admired people in the twentieth century;

[133] Donohue, "Hating Mother Teresa."
[134] Larivée, Chénard, and Sénéchal, "The Dark Side of Mother Teresa," 327.

it listed eighteen men and women from all over the world. At the top of the list was Mother Teresa. That may not justify sainthood, but it sure explains why she is so loved. It also suggests that her critics never laid a glove on her.

About the Author

Bill Donohue is president and CEO of the Catholic League for Religious and Civil Rights. He holds a Ph.D. in sociology from New York University. A former Bradley Resident Scholar at the Heritage Foundation, Bill served for two decades on the board of directors of the National Association of Scholars. He is the author of several books on civil liberties, social issues, and Catholicism.

Sophia Institute

Sophia Institute is a nonprofit institution that seeks to nurture the spiritual, moral, and cultural life of souls and to spread the Gospel of Christ in conformity with the authentic teachings of the Roman Catholic Church.

Sophia Institute Press fulfills this mission by offering translations, reprints, and new publications that afford readers a rich source of the enduring wisdom of mankind.

Sophia Institute also operates two popular online Catholic resources: CrisisMagazine.com and CatholicExchange.com.

Crisis Magazine provides insightful cultural analysis that arms readers with the arguments necessary for navigating the ideological and theological minefields of the day. *Catholic Exchange* provides world news from a Catholic perspective as well as daily devotionals and articles that will help you to grow in holiness and live a life consistent with the teachings of the Church.

In 2013, Sophia Institute launched Sophia Institute for Teachers to renew and rebuild Catholic culture through service to Catholic education. With the goal of nurturing the spiritual, moral, and cultural life of souls, and an abiding respect for the role and work of teachers, we strive to provide materials and programs that are at once enlightening to the mind and ennobling to the heart; faithful and complete, as well as useful and practical.

Sophia Institute gratefully recognizes the Solidarity Association for preserving and encouraging the growth of our apostolate over the course of many years. Without their generous and timely support, this book would not be in your hands.

www.SophiaInstitute.com
www.CatholicExchange.com
www.CrisisMagazine.com
www.SophiaInstituteforTeachers.org

Sophia Institute Press® is a registered trademark of Sophia Institute.
Sophia Institute is a tax-exempt institution as defined by the
Internal Revenue Code, Section 501(c)(3). Tax I.D. 22-2548708.